e-learning

An introductory workbook for staff in post-16 education

This workbook is based on an earlier edition written by Alison Page and Kevin Donovan and published by NIACE in 2005. This edition has been revised by Kevin Donovan.

niace

promoting adult learning

©2005 National Institute of Adult Continuing Education
(England and Wales)
Second edition 2006

21 De Montfort Street
Leicester
LE1 7GE

Company registration no. 2603322
Charity registration no. 1002775

NIACE has a broad remit to promote lifelong learning opportunities for adults. NIACE works
to develop increased participation in education and training, particularly for those who do
not have easy access because of class, gender, age, race, language and culture, learning
difficulties or disabilities, or insufficient financial resources.

You can find NIACE online at www.niace.org.uk

Cataloguing in Publication Data
A CIP record of this title is available from the British Library

Designed and typeset by Patrick Armstrong Book Production Services, London
Printed and bound in the UK by Cromwell Press, Trowbridge

ISBN 1 86201 253 9 / 978 1 86201 2530

Contents

Introduction

> **What is e-learning?**
> Simply, it means using digital technology (whether that's computers, the Internet, digital cameras, mobile phones etc.) in teaching and learning. You can find more detailed explanations and examples later in the book.

This book is for teachers, tutors, trainers and lecturers working in post-16 education and training. (See later for definitions of what we mean by this. Most of the time in this book we'll use the term 'tutor' as shorthand for the whole range of staff involved.) Its purpose is to help staff make greater use of e-learning to support their work. Some readers of this book will be new to e-learning. Others will have extensive experience. Wherever you are along this spectrum, you will be able to use this book to increase the effective use of technology in your teaching.

The ideas and information in this book are based on more than a decade of research and practice in e-learning. A very wide range of research studies and academic papers have been reviewed and summarised, and used to develop recommendations to help you in your work. Everyone involved in the development of this book has practical experience of teaching adults, and using e-learning techniques. e-learning is an accepted and fundamental part of the education scene and is a key element of professional practice. Government policy and the work of agencies like NIACE have given e-learning a higher profile and greater importance. Wherever you live or work you will have seen the influence of technology; teaching and learning are no different.

Staff in post-16 education and training – people like you – are a diverse group, with a wide range of needs and strengths. You are probably used to working with quite a degree of autonomy, and coping with a range of problems through your own efforts and creative thinking. This book is designed to fit in with the philosophy and needs of the sector by:

> **Putting you in control.** This book is non-prescriptive. It offers suggestions, and sources of information. It does not tell you what to do.

> **Inviting your participation**. Throughout this book you will find opportunities to take the work further and to undertake activities of one kind or another. The extent to which you follow through with these suggestions is up to you.

> **Offering flexible solutions**. In general, in education, there is no 'one size fits all' solution. This is particularly true in the post-16 sector, where there is so much diversity. This book aims to offer flexible and adaptable applications for e-learning, which you can tailor to fit your individual needs, and the needs of your learners.

For these reasons you can use the publication in any way you like, and read it in any order. You can start at the front and work through, or you can follow the cross-links between sections, which will take you on a range of routes through the material and lead you to information and resources elsewhere.

It would help your productive use of this book if you have easy access to the Internet as we give you lots of links to various Internet sites. You can type in these links in your Internet ('web') browser, and look at the sites. Some of them have a lot of material to help you.

There are pages and space at the end of the book for you to write in your own findings and opinions. We've put all such pages at the end so that you can photocopy them more easily and use them over again, or with other colleagues – or with your learners.

Inevitably there is some use of technical terms and jargon in the book so, as well as providing details of some 'jargon buster' resources, we have tried to explain terms we use as we go along or in the definitions section at the end of the book.

We give lots of references to useful Internet (or 'web') pages. Occasionally when you get there you will need to type the information you're seeking into a 'search' box and click a button to find it on the website.

Who are you?

This workbook is for anyone in the post-16 sector of education and training who wants to introduce an element of 'e-learning' into their work. We are assuming it will be of most use to teachers, lecturers, tutors, trainers – it doesn't really matter what title you have; we use the term 'tutor' most often – who work directly with learners or trainees – again the term isn't important. And by 'post-16' we mean further education colleges, adult and community learning, offender learning and skills, work-place learning and training – anything that isn't in a school or university (although staff in both those sectors might find the book useful).

So what is this 'e-learning'?

e-learning is a general term for the use of new technology in education. Some people use the phrase 'information and learning technology' (ILT) to mean the same thing. What's 'new' technology can quickly seem very old-fashioned, as this area changes all the time. But it includes computers (personal computers - PCs - and laptops), and the technology that connects computers and people together (in particular email and the Internet – also called the World

Wide Web, or simply 'the Web'). It also includes the various domestic technologies, like mobile phones, digital cameras and digital TV. New technologies like these – and lots of others – can be used by tutors and by learners to improve learning.

However e-learning should not mean the replacement of tutors by computers! There are some contexts (for example short technical courses including those aimed at a wide geographical spread of learners) where it does work to have only 'online' learning. But in fact, as you will find out, everyone involved in e-learning agrees that the most important parts of the e-learning process are the contributions of the tutor and the learner. What we are describing in this book is effective teaching and learning made even better by using technology in appropriate ways.

e-learning can be very high-tech. But it doesn't have to be. This book covers a wide range of types of e-learning, simple and more complex. We are assuming that, by reading and using this book, you are showing your enthusiasm to find out and become more involved in e-learning. We do give a lot of references to information available on the World Wide Web, so you will get most out of this book if you have access to the Internet.

Other terms are also used instead of e-learning, or while talking about e-learning. There are some definitions of these key terms on page **33**. In the box below you will see the first of the linked cross-references in this book. Follow the link now if you want to look at the list of terms. Otherwise, carry on reading this page.

What do all these technical terms mean? go to page 33

A lot of research has been done into e-learning. You probably don't have time to read everything that has been published. Instead this book will condense the main facts, and allow you to follow up any themes which interest you. This frees up your time to spend on applying e-learning as much or as little as you feel appropriate to your own professional circumstances.

There's a full set of references in the book directing you to further information, should you so wish.

Your participation

This book encourages you to participate. You don't have to be a passive reader. In order to participate you can:

> read the ideas presented here, and make up your own mind about the uses of e-learning;

> find out more about particular areas of interest, by following the links and reading selected material to which we provide references;

> think of ways to expand your use of e-learning, by borrowing some of the ideas presented in this book;

> use the short questionnaires (and quizzes, referred to elsewhere) to test your own opinions an development;

> become more involved, by joining online communities (more on those later), or producing and sharing your own ideas and materials with colleagues in your area of expertise.

The extent to which you want to participate is up to you. If it suits your own style of learning, you can make notes throughout this book, and carry out the tasks as you wish.

The building blocks of e-learning

e-learning doesn't just happen. For it to work, at least three building blocks need to be in place, each depending on the next.

> **Potential**: There must be some access to a technical foundation, for example computer equipment, which has the potential to support learning.

> **Possibility**: There must be creative possibilities, ways to make use of that potential to support learning.

> **Practice**: And there must be a teaching professional, using this potential, and realising these possibilities, in their teaching practice.

The diagram below shows how it works.

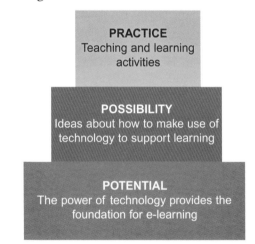

If any of the building blocks are missing then e-learning will not be a success. In this book you can support your professional practice by ensuring that you understand the possibilities for making use of the technical potential.

This book will allow you to investigate all three areas of interest. You can read them in any order that you like. See below for a related 'map' of the book's contents.

The shape of this book

This book has an introduction, followed by three further sections covering the three building blocks of e-learning. You can read these sections in any order that you like. This 'map' of the book might help you to find the section you want to read first.

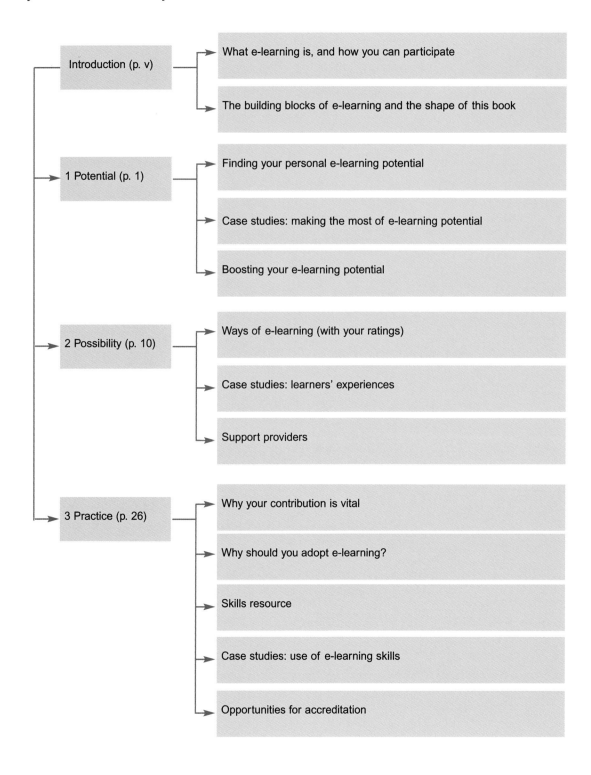

1

Potential

If you don't know where to start with e-learning, if you wonder what some of the technical and specialist words mean, if you think your own access to technology is limited, or if you want to boost your and your learners' e-learning potential, then this is the section to read first.

Before you can make use of e-learning, you need to be aware of what is available to you. In this section we will look at the potential that technology offers. Of course, the potential of technology is changing all the time and the circumstances in which you find yourself can vary. For this reason, in this section we try to suggest the broad scope of technological potential, and show how you can begin to utilise e-learning no matter how much or how little access you have to the wide choice of resources.

Here is a map of this section of the book.

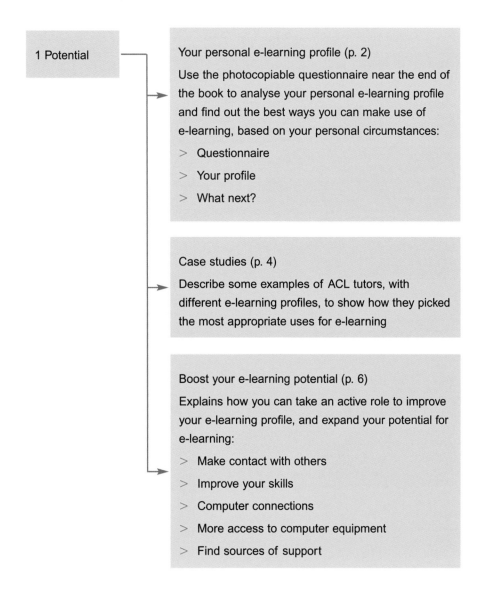

1 Potential

Your personal e-learning profile (p. 2)

Use the photocopiable questionnaire near the end of the book to analyse your personal e-learning profile and find out the best ways you can make use of e-learning, based on your personal circumstances:

> Questionnaire

> Your profile

> What next?

Case studies (p. 4)

Describe some examples of ACL tutors, with different e-learning profiles, to show how they picked the most appropriate uses for e-learning

Boost your e-learning potential (p. 6)

Explains how you can take an active role to improve your e-learning profile, and expand your potential for e-learning:

> Make contact with others

> Improve your skills

> Computer connections

> More access to computer equipment

> Find sources of support

You can try out some other self-assessments to establish your e-learning profile. One is based on the first edition of this book and can be found at **http://www.rsc-northwest.ac.uk/acl/PersonalProfile/index.htm.**

It's produced by a regional support centre (RSC) and you can find out more about RSCs later in the book.

Another self-assessment tool is being developed by the LSN (Learning and Skills Network). See **http://www.learningtechnologies.ac.uk/tools_services.asp?area=4**

Your personal e-learning profile

Find your e-learning profile

The 'building blocks' diagram on page vii showed that e-learning depends on the potential offered by technology. However, this potential varies greatly with individual circumstances: for example some tutors have plenty of easy access to a lot of computer facilities; some have much less access.

There are three key messages to bear in mind:

> Everyone in the UK has some access to computers and the Internet, because there is provision in public libraries and various 'online centres'.

> Even with very little direct access to some technologies it is possible to make use of e-learning.

> There is more to e-learning than computers.

For examples of online centres see

http://www.ufi.com/ukol/default.asp in England,
http://www.walesontheweb.org/cayw/index/en/00 0/078 in Wales,
http://www.learndirect.co.uk/personal/centres/ in Northern Ireland,
http://www.learndirectscotland.com/Where/ in Scotland.

The book concentrates on the use of computers, rather than some other technologies, in e-learning – although we will give you lots of references to these other applications. That's because computers are what most people associate with e-learning – and there are a lot of them about! So we sometimes use 'computers' as a proxy for a range of technologies. As you become more comfortable with e-learning you will begin to take a wider view of e-learning. And that's how it should be – effective e-learning means using whatever technologies work best for you and your learners.

There are many different factors which will influence the use you make of e-learning. We have put together some of the most important factors to create a personal 'e-learning profile'. Use the photocopiable questionnaire on page 37 to discover your e-learning profile. Once you have done this you can:

> evaluate your possibilities for e-learning;

> find out how to boost your e-learning profile.

You can also read some case studies to find out how different e-learning profiles enable different types of e-learning.

So now I know my e-learning profile: what next?

Once you have used the questionnaire and given answers to establish your e-learning profile you can make better use of the information in this book. You can relate everything that you read to your personal circumstances, and select options that are particularly relevant to you.

And remember you aren't stuck with your current e-learning profile forever. There are actions you can take to improve any aspect of your e-learning profile. The next section of this book will give you some advice about ways to boost your profile.

Decide what you want to do next:

Read the case studies, which give examples of different tutors with different learning profiles. The case studies demonstrate how each e-learning profile suggests a different approach to e-learning. If you try the questionnaire to produce your own profile, you'll see how the profiles for our three case studies were produced.

Case studies – go to page 4

Improve your e-learning profile, by taking actions that boost your potential in areas where you have a low score.

Improve your e-learning profile – go to page 6

Look at some ideas which have been developed for uses of e-learning, and find the ones which match your e-learning profile.

Ways of e-learning – go to page 11

Case studies: different e-learning profiles

Jill

Jill is a yoga tutor. She teaches in a local sports and recreation centre. Her current class consists of mainly older people.

Jill's e-learning profile

e-learning potential	Low	Moderate	High	Very high
1 Personal	a	b	c	d
2 Learner	a	b	c	d
3 Institutional	a	b	c	d
4 Skills	a	b	c	d

Jill's partner is a web designer and her daughter is a computer engineer; at home she has access to a high-specification computer with a broadband connection. The family has lots of other digital equipment. She has never been on a computer course, but she has picked up a lot of skills by using the computer with her family. However, there are no computers for her to use at the recreation centre and most of her learners have no computer at home.

e-learning verdict

Jill can make the most of the facilities at home to prepare for classes and to support her own professional development. She can research the style of yoga in which she specialises, and perhaps learn more about other styles. She can prepare high-quality handouts for her learners, and print them out to provide them in paper format. She can use the family digital video camera to film learners to show them their strengths and weaknesses. Jill can also look for online communities, such as mailing lists, where she can gain support and share ideas with other yoga tutors.

Carlos

Carlos is a creative writing tutor and published author. He has no computer at home and little interest in technology.

Carlos's e-learning profile

e-learning potential	Low	Moderate	High	Very high
1 Personal	a	b	c	d
2 Learner	a	b	c	d
3 Institutional	a	b	c	d
4 Skills	a	b	c	d

Carlos writes in longhand; a friend types up his manuscripts. He teaches in a university annexe where there is a resource centre with a limited number of computers. He teaches classes of mainly young professionals, and virtually all his learners have access to computers at home.

e-learning verdict

Carlos can ask his learners to word-process their home assignments. This has the advantage of simplifying and speeding up the process of revision and correction, which is so important to improving writing quality. Learners can use digital cameras to take photos to illustrate their writing and insert these in their texts. He could also ask the university resource centre to give him an email address, and tell his learners to send him their assignments electronically, a couple of days before the weekly session. He can go to the resource centre, pick up his email and print out the assignments. This means he would be ready with feedback in advance of the lesson.

Geoff

Geoff is a full-time basic skills tutor at a community college. He has recently taken an in-service e-learning development course. His college has invested in technology resources.

Geoff's e-learning profile

e-learning potential	Low	Moderate	High	Very high
1 Personal	a	b	c	d
2 Learner	a	b	c	d
3 Institutional	a	b	c	d
4 Skills	a	b	c	d

Geoff's learners are from a variety of backgrounds, and many have low incomes and little access to technology outside of the classroom. However, Geoff and his learners have access to a good range of classroom facilities, including basic skills teaching materials for use on computers.

e-learning potential

Geoff can select hardware (i.e. computers in this case) and software (i.e. computer applications like word-processing or learning materials for the computer) from the range available to him. He has to think carefully about the strengths and weakness of the software on offer, and build the use of this material into his pedagogical practice in the classroom. It would be a mistake to rely on the software available without backing it up with good teaching support for his learners. In the end Geoff picks individual exercises from three different packages of learning material, and combines them during the year with other teaching and learning options.

Helen

Helen is a full-time electrical installation tutor based in a work-based training centre. She is keen to maximise the use of technology for record-keeping but acknowledges that this is a fast-changing scene and she doesn't know everything and needs to keep up-to-date. The centre has a good range of technology resources and a sophisticated management information system and virtual learning environment.

Helen's e-learning profile

e-learning potential	Low	Moderate	High	Very high
1 Personal	a	b	c	d
2 Learner	a	b	c	d
3 Institutional	a	b	c	d
4 Skills	a	b	c	d

Helen's trainees sit 'on-line' assessments and tests at the end of each module of their course and record their progress electronically as they go. They are fairly 'technology-savvy' and all have mobile phones.

e-learning potential

Helen can select software systems such as 'e-portfolios' for her trainees to use. This means they can input all their achievements (and use a variety of media to do so) and use the portfolio as a developing curriculum vitae – as well as proof of achievement. She can send text messages simultaneously to all trainees to keep them informed of course developments when they are in various 'off-site' locations. Visits by NVQ assessors are less fraught as evidence is to hand and can be examined more constructively than with the old paper-based systems. Helen is keen to develop this area of activity further and plans to help all her colleagues and all of their trainees to maximise electronic record-keeping and usage.

Boost your e-learning potential

If you have read this section so far you will have a good understanding of the potential of e-learning for a tutor. You will probably have recognised that your present circumstances offer you many options for using e-learning.

However, you can take things further, if you want to. This sub-section is where you can do something active to boost your e-learning potential, and thus improve your e-learning profile. This will expand the range of e-learning options which are available to you.

You don't have to take any of these actions if you don't want to. However, if you do, you can enrich the possibilities for yourself and your learners.

Some of the things you can do (pages 6–9):

> make contact with other tutors;

> improve your skills;

> boost your connectivity;

> increase your access to ICT;

> discover useful learning materials;

> find other sources of support.

Make contact with other tutors

It will be clear by now, if you didn't know this already, that using technology is a great way to find and share. That is clear from the amazing amount of time people spend on the Internet, using Google to search for information, and from the popularity of mail lists and 'blogs'. This means it is also a very effective way for people to learn and develop together and to share what they know and can do. And that includes tutors. The Community Learning Resource is an example of collaboration designed for staff in the post-16 sector. It includes a service called the Apollo discussion group, which allows you to communicate by email with other tutors who, for example, already have, or are currently developing, e-learning materials for their learners.

Apollo (which stands for Adult Practitioners' On-Line Learning Opportunities) is for the use of tutors so that they can discuss ideas about teaching and learning. This could include anything – from opinions about the website, to debates on creating professional practice communities, and information and ideas on developing e-learning content. In particular, it is an opportunity for staff who participate to share experiences and offer mutual support, information and guidance.

If you specialise in teaching numeracy, literacy or ESOL, there is also a forum (another term for an online discussion group) within the ELNET 'online community resource for teachers'.

Apollo online discussion
http://www.aclearn.net/communicate/discussion

The ELNET online community resource
http://www.elnet.org.uk/

What is a mailing list? – read more on page 30.

Of course, you can also meet in more traditional ways! You can discuss e-learning with colleagues in your own organisation or local area and there are many other opportunities to get together and to network with other tutors informally or at events of various kinds. We have included some of these in the next section on improving your skills. You could even organise a meeting or event if you feel there's a need; we've included a reference to a guide which tells you how to do just that.

Improve your skills

There is a wide range of courses in almost all parts of the UK, designed to develop computer and other technology skills. Improving your understanding of computer technology will automatically boost your e-learning profile. Good places to start would be local colleges and community centres (perhaps the place where you teach) or learndirect (which offers distance learning in basic and intermediate computer skills, among many other courses).

As well as improving your computer skills you may wish to investigate training and development designed specifically to support e-learning and the better use of information and learning technology by tutors. Such professional development support is offered by NIACE (National Institute for Adult Continuing Education), LSN (Learning and Skills Network)

and other providers. Further details are given in the boxes below. Lots of sector organisations run useful events where you can find out more and meet fellow professionals.

There have been lots of initiatives to discover the related training needs of tutors, and details can be found in some of the links below. For example NIACE has investigated the training implications of having 'ICT' as a skill for life and has recommended the ITQ (IT user qualification) as a way to improve technology skills and the eCPD (e-learning continuing professional development) framework as the best way to support the development of e-learning know-how.

There are regional support centres (RSCs) with technical, training and curriculum specialists in Scotland, Northern Ireland, Wales and England. We've included details of these later and within the section on support providers.

The possible list of resources and contacts to help you improve your skills is endless. These are just some.

You (and your learners) can get advice from
http://www.nextstep.org.uk/
http://www.niace.org.uk/projects/learningfromexperience/

Relevant courses and qualifications can be found at
http://www.learndirect-advice.co.uk/findacourse/
http://www.learndirect.co.uk or 0800 100 900 in England, Wales and Northern Ireland
http://www.learndirectscotland.com/ in Scotland

Details of the ITQ can be found at **http://itq.e-skills.com**
Some examples of subject-related support for using the ITQ are at
http://www.learningtechnologies.ac.uk/subject_specific.asp?area=57

NIACE has developed an online staff development e-learning centre (SDELC) and there are more details on this later. Part of this is the E-Guides staff development programme, which has been designed to support adult and community learning staff to embed the use of e-learning across the curriculum. The programme covers the use of any technology to both support and enhance all teaching and learning. SDELC is at **http://www.aclearn.net/sdelc**

Events
http://www.learningtechnologies.ac.uk/ for the UK
http://www.ltscotland.org.uk/ictineducation/professionaldevelopment/Events.asp in Scotland
http://www.aclearn.net

Resources
NIACE was one of the partners in the 'exploring e-learning' programme. This was aimed primarily at teachers of numeracy, literacy and ESOL, but its resources are useful to a wide range of practitioners and are still available at **http://www.elnet.org.uk/**
and see **http://www.learningtechnologies.ac.uk/learning_materials.asp?area=59**

E-Guides information is at **http://www.aclearn.net/skills/e-guides**

Details of the eCPD framework are at **http://www.learningtechnologies.ac.uk/skills.asp?area=2**

Boost your connectivity

Much of the information in this book is based on having access to the Internet, where you can find and share information, as well as do everything else which the 'web' offers, like booking holidays, downloading music, sending email, displaying photographs, or using a personal 'blog' (a web log) to tell the world what you or your learners have been doing.

Many of these Internet services require the right kind of computer, and adequate telecommunications power, often referred to as 'broadband'. This allows you to have high-speed Internet access, and in such a way that telephone calls and a permanent Internet connection can share a single phone line simultaneously. You may have this at home; you can check whether the technology would work where you live by using one of the links below.

If you have responsibility for the technology, computer and connectivity systems in your organisation, you will wish to maximise the associated benefits for colleagues and learners. There are organisations which offer help. Try the links given in this section. If you don't have this responsibility, you might want to pass on this information to the people in charge of technical services for your place of work.

JANET JANET is the private, government-funded network dedicated to the needs of education. It connects the UK's education and research organisations to each other, as well as to the rest of the world, through links to the global Internet. All further and higher education organisations are connected to JANET, as are all the Research Councils.

As we've noted elsewhere (and see below) learners can access new technology in lots of places other than when they are with you, for example in public libraries. But many of them – and possibly you – will also perhaps have a 'wireless laptop'. This is a laptop computer which can access the Internet from a wireless 'hotspot'. There are now lots of these – in railway stations, cafes and restaurants, bars, cinemas and other places. You might want to establish with your learners just who has access to this technology and where it can be used in your area.

> There is more about JANET at **http://www.ja.net**
> The JISC regional support centres (RSCs) help institutions with JANET network issues and offer other technical support. They are at **http://www.jiscmail.ac.uk/help/rsc.htm**
>
> Find out about broadband at **http://www.filesaveas.com/broadband.html**
>
> You can find where broadband is available at various Internet sites including **http://www.bt.com**
>
> You can find your local wireless hotspots at **http://www.wifinder.com/**
>
> The terminology is explained by various 'jargon busters' including at **http//:www.ltscotland.org.uk/ictineducation/jargonbuster/index.asp**

Increase your access to ICT

In principle, everyone in the UK has access to the technology that underpins e-learning, via their local UK online centre. So, if you or your learners don't have computers at home or in your organisation, there should be somewhere within easy reach where you can use computers.

 'UK online centres aim to ensure that everyone in the UK who wants it will have access to computers, Internet and email near to where they live. You can use a computer to access useful information, keep up with the kids, find a job, or even shop online – our helpful staff are on hand to give you as much support as you need.

Visiting a UK online centre means you can explore the opportunities that new technologies offer, such as further learning and updating your skills. UK online centres work closely with learndirect centres and other learning venues to provide lots of different ways to build on your learning.' (UK centres).

But, as we note elsewhere, 'new' technology is more than computers. Mobile phones, digital cameras – and the remote control handset for your television – offer ways of communicating with others and finding information.

To find out more about UK Online centres see
http://www.ufi.com/ukol/default.asp in England,
http://www.walesontheweb.org/cayw/index/en/000/078
in Wales,
http://www.learndirect.co.uk/personal/centres/ in
Northern Ireland,
http://www.learndirectscotland.com/Where/ in
Scotland

Information about using digital television is at
http://www.bbc.co.uk/reception/digital_tv/index.shtml

Find other sources of support

Organisations and initiatives that offer
support for e-learning are listed on pages
21–5.

2

Possibility

In this section you can find out about some of the possibilities for using e-learning in your practice as a teacher or trainer. These are ideas that have been developed and tested by teaching professionals all over the world. As a practitioner, you may have no experience of using e-learning, or you might have a range of e-learning options with which you are comfortable and familiar. In either case you could be surprised by the wide range of additional e-learning options that are possible for someone in your circumstances.

Here you can rate these ideas and record your decisions about which are right for you. These decisions should not be set in stone, and you might find yourself coming back to this section as your confidence increases.

You will also find out about the resources that are available to support your use of e-learning in your work.

Here is a map of this section.

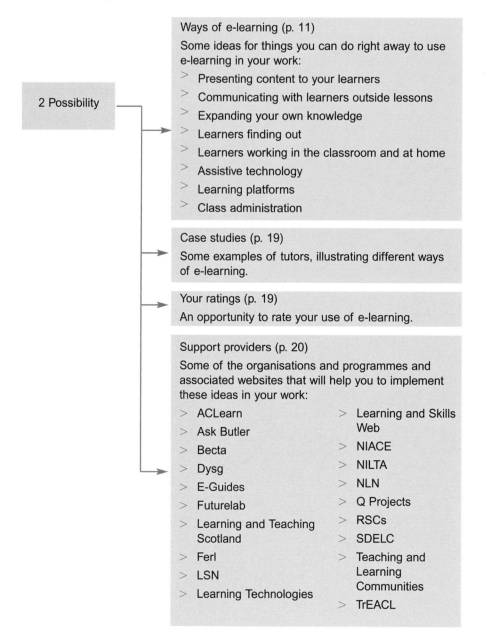

2 Possibility

Ways of e-learning (p. 11)
Some ideas for things you can do right away to use e-learning in your work:
> Presenting content to your learners
> Communicating with learners outside lessons
> Expanding your own knowledge
> Learners finding out
> Learners working in the classroom and at home
> Assistive technology
> Learning platforms
> Class administration

Case studies (p. 19)
Some examples of tutors, illustrating different ways of e-learning.

Your ratings (p. 19)
An opportunity to rate your use of e-learning.

Support providers (p. 20)
Some of the organisations and programmes and associated websites that will help you to implement these ideas in your work:
> ACLearn
> Ask Butler
> Becta
> Dysg
> E-Guides
> Futurelab
> Learning and Teaching Scotland
> Ferl
> LSN
> Learning Technologies
> Learning and Skills Web
> NIACE
> NILTA
> NLN
> Q Projects
> RSCs
> SDELC
> Teaching and Learning Communities
> TrEACL

Ways of e-learning

There are many different ways to use e-learning. In this section you will find out about a wide range of different possibilities, tried and tested methods that have been used by educational professionals in a wide range of contexts. You are certain to find some ideas here that you can use right away.

If you have investigated your e-learning profile (see page 37), you will have a better idea of which approaches are realistic options for you. Some of the ideas in this section will apply to your circumstances right now, and others will be within your reach with a little help. Use the information in this book to:

> find possibilities that you can use immediately;

> think about possibilities for the future;

> make use of the support available to help you to turn these possibilities into reality.

Things you can do

E-learning can help you with all of the following activities:

Supporting your teaching (pages 11–15)

> Presenting content to your learners

> Communicating with your learners outside of lessons

> Expanding your own knowledge

Supporting your learners (pages 15–17)

> Learners finding out

> Learners working in the classroom

> Learners working at home

> Assistive technology /support for special needs

Organising and managing your work (pages 17–18)

> Learning platforms

> Class administration

Read the following pages for more detail about each of these options. Many would also argue – and some research (see later) supports them – that e-learning also helps to improve participation, retention and achievement – and the quality of teaching and learning. This may be because the excitement of having access to new technology can motivate learners to come to an organisation and to perform better. It may also help tutors to focus again on the resources they use and their methods of teaching and training.

> Some of the evidence about the positive impact of e-learning can be found at websites such as **http://www.niace.org.uk/Research/ICT/WON.htm** **http://www.learningtechnologies.ac.uk** and (for example) from the Becta review at **http://www.becta.org.uk/**

Presenting content to your learners

Technology, including computers and other equipment, can be used to help you present content to learners in your lessons. The way you do this will depend on what facilities are available where you work. Check your e-learning profile to see which applies to you:

> **If there are no technology facilities where you work** – can you prepare your handouts at home, for example using word-processing software, your digital camera, graphics packages etc.?

> **If there is a computer with a projector** – prepare and give presentations using PowerPoint or a similar package, as a potentially creative alternative to 'chalk and talk' or other teaching methods.

> **If there are computers connected by a network** – you can share handouts, presentations and other information over the network, so each learner can see the content on their own computer. Your learners will also be able to use specially designed learning materials (shared, bought, acquired free and/or produced by you and other colleagues).

An additional facility to explore is an interactive whiteboard. At its simplest such a board will display content that you have developed, but it also allows you and your learners to input data (for example by writing on the whiteboard) which then goes into the computer. It's like a (very) intelligent flip chart.

For more information about interactive whiteboards go to page 30

Other ideas:

> **File sharing** – Share computer files in
electronic form with your learners. Then they
can work interactively with copies of your
files. For example, give them a document
which is incomplete (a story with no ending, a
passage of writing with words blanked out, a
paragraph with alternative words to use) and
ask them to finish it. Material like this – and
much more – is also available form the sources
referred to later in the book.

> **CD content** – A CD writer, which allows you
to copy text, pictures or sounds onto a CD, is
not expensive these days; in fact most modern
personal computers (PCs) have one already
built in. Blank CDs are relatively cheap – so
you could copy onto a CD all the material
which you plan to use with a class during the
term or the year. A lot of learning material for
use on computers comes on a CD (sometimes
free on the cover of magazines).

> **Multiple media** – Expand your use of
photographs, film clips, sounds and
animations. Content like this is often available
on the Internet or on CDs which may be less
expensive than textbooks. And here is where

you can be more creative in using technology:
digital cameras, mobile phones, MP3 music
players and games machines all allow you and
your learners to store, view and share multiple
media. So learners could collect material for a
research assignment on a camera and bring it
back (or email it) to show the class via a
computer.

Lots of other materials to use – and ideas on how
to use them – can be found, for examples only, via
http://ww.aclearn.net
http://www.nln.ac.uk/materials/
http://www.learningtechnologies.ac.uk
http://www.elnet.org.uk
http://www.ltscotland.org.uk
http://www.teachingandlearning.org.uk/
http://www.jisc.ac.uk

If you intend to try producing your own e-learning
materials, have a look at
**http://www.niace.org.uk/Publications/D/Develop
ingElearning.asp** and
http://ferl.becta.org.uk/display.cfm?page=419

In every case you must take care that you are not
infringing copyright law and regulations. You can
find out more at **http://www.becta.org.uk/**

The advantages of creating e-learning content

> **Higher quality** – Content prepared on and for computers is usually clearer, and more attractive than handwritten notes. Unless your writing is very neat, your learners may find word-processed documents easier to use.

> **Learning** – As you know, learners learn best in all sorts of ways, and not always by the written word. Pictures and sounds – and links to other places – can make teaching more imaginative and learning more productive.

> **Save time** – You can reuse content more easily if it is kept on your computer. It is also easy to adapt old content, and to take useful bits and pieces from old material when you want to put together something new.

> **Wider range** – You can give your learners access to a wider range of content if you expand your lessons to include e-learning. The only consideration is what might be useful to you in getting across the skills, knowledge and ideas that you want to convey. Electronic content does not replace the human face of teaching, but it is another resource that the teaching professional can draw upon. A foreign field trip may be too expensive for your learners – but you can visit and explore 'virtually'.

Communicating with learners outside of lessons

Connectivity can be used to help the tutor keep in touch with learners outside of lessons. The most common way to do this is to send email messages to learners. Remember: communication is two-way; you can also use email to let your learners communicate with you, for pastoral care, for example, or as a way of handing in homework.

Check your e-learning profile, to see what type of communication will suit your class:

> **If learner access is good** – If you and your learners all have access to email, then there is no reason not to use it to help with the business of running the course. You can send out information, set assignments and receive completed work. If you think your learners

won't have computer access, double-check first: how many of your learners' households have a computer, Internet access or digital TV?

> **If there is some access in the institution** – Investigate whether your organisation has a learning centre or other computer facilities available to learners. Then you can send email messages to them, knowing that everyone will have the chance to pick the message up during the week.

> **Limited facilities** – If you can't be confident that all your learners can access email, then it isn't appropriate to make email usage central to the course. However, you could keep the possibility open for learners who would prefer to give in homework by email.

> **Text messaging** on a mobile phone also provides a way to keep in touch with learners outside of class times. It is possible to send messages (e.g. reminders about submitting work, timetable changes) to large numbers of learners at once. As with all other forms of electronic communication, make sure that you do not disadvantage learners who do not have access.

As well as checking your own e-learning profile and your skills at using various bits of technology, you may need to run or organise some training for your learners so that they are familiar with the resources you plan to use.

Other ideas

> **A mailing list** – A mailing list is a facility to share emails with a list of named recipients. Any email sent to the list could be read by everyone on it. It's a good way to extend discussions outside the classroom, and build a friendly learning community, particularly if you only meet occasionally as a class.

To find out about mailing lists go to page 30

> **A tutor website** – If you have the skills and experience you could set up your own website. Learners could go there to download materials, or you could keep a list of links to useful Internet sites. Some tutors produce blogs (short for web logs). These are like online journals that can be updated as often as you like. You could use these to offer week-by-week up-to-date content to your learners.

There are ideas about using blogs for teaching and learning in various places including
http://elgg.leeds.ac.uk/edublog/weblog/

Find out about creating your own blog at
**http://www.livejournal.com or
http://www.blogger.com/start or
http://www.educause.edu**

> **A wiki** – this is a website created by a group of collaborators.

Find out about wikis at
http://wiki.org/wiki.cgi?WhatIsWiki

You can find ideas about using wikis at
http://ferl.becta.org.uk

> **An intranet site** – some organisations will have an 'intranet' or a 'learning platform' (otherwise known as a 'virtual learning environment' or VLE – or 'virtual classroom'). This is an electronic area (on the organisation's computer network system) where materials can be stored and accessed – and much more. There's information about all this later.

The advantages

Speed of communication is an important reason for using some of the tools above. It also means being able to keep in touch with learners who may be widely scattered and only come together once a week for a couple of hours.

Can you suggest other advantages of electronic communication? (Try the worksheet near the end of the book. You could also use this with your learners.) Some possible reasons are contained in the sections below.

Expanding your own knowledge

There is always more for you to learn about your specialist area. You may work in a field where up-to-date knowledge is changing rapidly, such as current affairs or science. You may work in a field where there are a wide range of opinions and theories, such as philosophy or history. Or you may work in a field where there are lots of grass-

roots practitioners or craftspeople, such as those working in jewellery making or furniture restoration, and each with something to contribute to a discussion about materials or techniques.

Online research can help you with all of these types of knowledge: up-to-date information, opinions and theories, and the experiences of practitioners.

Finding up-to-date information – go to page 14

Finding opinions and theories – go to page 15

Finding out about other practitioners – go to page 15

Up-to-date information

Information on the Internet can be completely up to date compared, say, with books. You can access the websites of newspapers, magazines and TV stations from all over the world. Some sites you might like to check out include the following:

> Newspapers maintain websites with news and opinions. A good approach is to check out the site of your favourite newspaper, and then a newspaper whose views you don't share. It's useful to collect information from both sides of a debate. You can find a huge range of items including cartoons, photos, letters from readers and statistical data. All of these might provide resources you can use to support learning. The Guardian's website, for example, has won awards for design and content and its use of technology.

The Guardian online is at
http://www.guardian.co.uk

> Broadcasting organisations have websites which are constantly being updated. They offer a news service as well as information arising from, or supporting, documentary and opinion programs. The BBC's website is regarded as a good example. For example – and you can find many others yourself – the BBC website included many resources linked to the award-winning TV series Planet Earth. These constitute an incredible resource for science, geography, sociology and current affairs courses. This is just one example of the range of material available on the BBC site to support a wide range of courses.

> BBC website: **http://www.bbc.co.uk**
> **http://www.bbc.co.uk/nature/animals/planetearth/**

> And remember the Internet is international, so you can access news sources from all over the world. This includes foreign language sites.

Opinions and theories

On the Internet you can find opinions and theories right across the spectrum, from the respectable to the wacky. This is where your own judgement comes into play. How reliable is the source? How mainstream is the point of view? Could your learners benefit from studying these opinions? Some types of sites you might like to check out include the following:

> University sites are maintained by a wide range of institutions, nationally and internationally. Some sites have more content than others. Some departments, and some individual academics, are very keen on using the Internet to spread their ideas. Take a look at the website of any academic institution that you respect. Talk to a friendly academic, and ask them to recommend any online resources in your areas of interest.

> Just a few examples of university research websites are: **http://www.gla.ac.uk/R-E/**
> **http://www.liv.ac.uk/research/rnri/**
> **http://www.bangor.ac.uk/research/**

> The site of an enthusiast or group of enthusiasts. People put an enormous effort into their enthusiasms. They collect information and offer strong opinions. You can find sites on almost any hobby, place, famous person, movement, period of history etc.

> An example of an enthusiast website:
> **http://www.allotments-uk.com/**

> The websites of pressure groups or charities obviously include both facts and opinions. They may be giving information or opinions, recruiting, raising money or publicising campaigns. The Internet is full of examples. We give just one.

> A charity website:
> **http://www.msf.org/unitedkingdom/**

Experiences of practitioners

The Internet can put you in touch with other practitioners in your field. Some sites you might like to check out are:

> **Professional association sites** Check the promotional literature of any professional association to which you belong; most have a website nowadays.

> Just one, in this case for physiotherapists, is **http://www.csp.org.uk/**

People offering services or products For example, if you are teaching a craft subject, you can look at the quality and style of products available in Britain and internationally.

> For example, the Wales Craft Council site is at **http://www.walescraftcouncil.co.uk/**

> **Websites created by other people teaching in your subject area (or by you)**

How can you find sites that might be useful to you? By looking in magazines and newspapers, by asking friends and colleagues, by connecting to well-respected sites like the BBC.

Another method is to use an Internet search engine. These are so important they have a section of their own in this book.

(Search engines – go to page 30)

Learners finding out

Just as you can find out new knowledge from the Internet, so can your learners. But there are more concerns when learners do research than when you do. For example:

> Are your learners mature and focused enough to concentrate on the job at hand, without getting distracted by unsuitable content?

> Are your learners experienced enough to discriminate between good and bad information?

> Do your learners have the skills to extract the information they need from lengthy or complex source documents?

The answers to these questions may be 'yes'. If you are not sure, then you can support your learners by monitoring their activity, giving them advice, and helping to develop their skills so that they are more discerning users of information. For learners who lack skill and confidence you may need to provide very controlled access to carefully vetted content.

At one end of the scale – strictly controlled access

Give your learners access to a single website, which you have checked in advance. You know exactly what they will find there and what learning outcomes you hope they will achieve.

At the other end of the scale – a free search

Mature and experienced learners may have the ability to carry out their own Internet searches, and evaluate the variable content that they find. There is more information about Internet search engines on page 30.

Somewhere in the middle – information skills

Give your learners links to two or three contrasting Internet sites. Ask them to investigate an issue or argument. Provide some questions to guide their work: What are the contrasting opinions presented in these sites? Which do you think is the most reliable? What evidence is presented to support the opinions?

And remember – your learners can do this research in a range of contexts:

> where you teach them, with you supervising;

> in a resource centre or library (schedule a class in that location) with supervision from yourself or support staff;

> in a resource centre or library outside of teaching time (if they can work without supervision);

> at home or at work, if that is possible.

Learners working as a class

Check your e-learning profile (page 37). Do your learners have access to computers in the room you use? If so, you can use these resources to help your learners to do their work. This is how most people envisage e-learning. Hopefully this book has begun to show you the many other ways in which ILT can support learning. However, where facilities allow it, the use of computers to support traditional learning activities remains a very important aspect of e-learning.

We have seen how learners can carry out research on the Internet, in a group when they are with you or otherwise. They can also make use of any software installed on the computers where you are teaching. The most typical example would be to use word-processing software to prepare text. Learners often appreciate the neat presentation, and the spelling check facility, which helps them to take pride in their work.

But don't be limited to word-processing. Databases, spreadsheets, graphics and presentation programmes might all be useful to you. And there may be specialist software to support your subject area. We give lots of examples and sources of information later on. For example you and your learners might want to create, adapt or share resources using various freely-accessible materials.

> Popular ways to produce materials in the ways described above – and below – include the use of Hot Potatoes software and web quests. You can find out more at
> **http://www.hotpotatoes.info/**
> and
> **http://www.webquestuk.org.uk/**

Learners working at home

Do your learners have access to computers outside the classroom? If so, they can use these resources to extend their learning outside formal lesson times. (And, some learners may be allowed to use computers at work.)

Of course there are some special concerns with the use of e-learning outside the classroom:

> It would be unfair to discriminate against learners who don't have access to computer resources at home. Be careful to consider all your learners when planning this type of activity. (But do they have other available technologies which they could use?)

> Make sure your learners have the technical and information skills they need to do the work. This is just as important as making sure they have access to the right equipment.

> Why not include e-learning as one of the many ways in which learners can tackle an assignment? For example learners could have the choice of doing research in the local library, on the Internet, or both. They could carry out an assignment by interviewing people and writing up the results – or they could take digital video or photographs of what they've discovered.

Some learners will be keen to use their home computers to complete set work. Try to be flexible and supportive enough to allow this, where feasible. This is another example where the professionalism and judgement of the individual tutor are vital.

Assistive technology

Assistive or adaptive technology involves using information and communications technology (ICT), and other technical solutions, to improve the ability of people with special educational needs to participate in educational activities. This may take two forms:

> The use of technology to enable learners with special needs to utilise ICT more readily. An example would be a system which reads out the text content of a website for users with visual difficulties.

> The use of technology to enable learners with special needs to participate in other learning activities, which may not be ICT based. An example would be the use of a voice synthesiser to enable learners with speech difficulties to join in a discussion.

Assistive technology is a potentially vast area, in which there is lots of specialist advice and information. Lead organisations for various forms of disability will offer advice on particular approaches from the perspective of users and their needs. Good sources of information are TechDis, AbiltyNet and the Foundation for Assistive Technology (FAST). TechDis also produce lots of downloadable packs of materials and guides for tutors.

FAST is at **http://www.fastuk.org/**

AbilityNet is at **http://www.abilitynet.org.uk/**

TechDis is at **http://www.techdis.ac.uk**

Learning platforms

'Learning platform' is a generic term covering a variety of different computer-based products, all of which support e-learning in some way. This includes learning made available via intranets, via the Internet and via a third party. Learning platforms can range from products which just provide learning material, to systems including a learner tracking system and a facility to enable users to create their own content, to more sophisticated systems which provide a selection of communications, learning content, assessment, tracking and other facilities. In brief, a learning platform in education and training can enable (in theory) the smoother management and administration of learning which includes e-learning.

Learning platforms are sometimes called 'learning management systems'. The terms also include specialist products: virtual learning environments (VLEs) and managed learning environments (MLEs) are software systems which manage learners' access to and use of learning materials.

As a tutor you will only be able to use VLEs and MLEs if the equipment and software are available where you work. You might like to find out about these systems because:

> they are becoming more common, and you may encounter them in the future;

> if you teach in an institution that offers these facilities you should be able to make an informed decision about whether to use them or not;

> if you have the responsibility to decide whether to invest in MLEs and VLEs, then you need to have a context for your decision.

If you don't think any of these apply to you, skip this short section.

So what are VLEs and MLEs?

A VLE provides the computer system which allows your learners to access electronic learning materials. For example a learner may log on to a VLE, and it may present him or her with a test, and then, as a result of the test, bring up on screen a lesson based on what information and skills the learner still has to learn. It may track the learner's progress against the set curriculum, and it may provide reports to the tutor. A VLE may provide your learners with a sequence of lessons, which the learners can work through, each at their own pace.

VLEs vary, but usually offer some basic functions. The advantages include freeing up the tutor to spend time on other activities, such as support for learners who need a lot of attention, and allowing all learners to progress at a speed that suits the individual. So it can be very useful for diverse groups of learners, and for classes that have need for a lot of support.

An MLE is a larger system that surrounds the VLE. An MLE links the classwork to a larger system, which might include learner registration, attendance, finance, and even data links to other institutions.

An intranet is a website which is exclusive to a group or an organisation.

You can find a 'jargon buster' and reports about the use of learning platforms on the ACLearn website. (See box in next column.)

Further information and background can be found via

http://www.aclearn.net

http://ferl.becta.org.uk

Some differences between systems are discussed on the Ferl website and you may like to read Becta's information (aimed at schools but useful) at **http://schools.becta.org.uk**

Read related JISC information at **http://www.jisc.ac.uk**

Class administration

Even in the absence of an MLE, your institution may offer some electronic support for the normal administrative tasks of a tutor. Examples might be a class list printed out from a computer learner record system, or a way to register attendance each week online, and send it automatically to the office or administrator. Generally this use of technology is not a matter of choice: the institution either requires it or does not support it.

But you can supplement any system with class records of your own, depending on your skill at using computer software. Many tutors use database and spreadsheet systems to keep class records, for example. This is a matter for your individual judgement. Computerised administration can help you to keep track of vital information, and it can reduce your administrative (or bureaucratic) workload.

Case studies: learners working with computers

Mohammed

Mohammed taught adults with moderate to severe learning difficulties, and limited language skills. He taught his learners to use a simple software package which let them create pictures on the computer screen.

Mohammed recorded an episode of the TV programme Art Attack onto video. The learners watched the programme, and then used the computer package to create pictures based on the examples of artwork they had seen on the video. With tutor support every learner was able to produce an original piece of creative work.

> See **http://www.hitentertainment.com/artattack/**

Margaret

Margaret taught a range of courses such as floristry and flower arranging. The products and assessment evidence of her learners were generally perishable and fragile.

Margaret used a digital camera to take pictures of her learners' work. She was able to print out copies of the photos from her laptop, for learners' portfolios. She also placed some of the most interesting examples on a class website. This was an acknowledgement of her learners' hard work, and provided examples for other classes to share.

> To inspire her learners even more, Margaret found a 'pod cast' about flower arranging from Woman's Hour **http://www.bbc.co.uk/radio4/womanshour/home_index.shtml** and she downloaded this to her computer.

Joan

Joan Pilkington, a tutor in lace-making for Derby Adult Learning Service, could never envisage how the use of IT or any modern technology could enhance the learning experience in her class: lace making and IT seemed to be poles apart. However, a random e-learning drop-in session started the ball rolling and she now regularly uses scanning equipment to highlight the intricate details in the lace which is often lost in conventional forms of photography.

> Joan now even feels confident enough to display the scanned images on the DerbyLearn learning platform, at **http://www.derbylearn.net** (case study taken from NIACE's Chips With Everything, Issue 11, March 2006)

The Internet is full of useful case studies. Try to find some more and relate them to your own experience.

Your ratings

How did you relate to all the ideas and information in the previous section? As you read through the ideas about applications of e-learning you may have been thinking 'I already knew that' or 'I could do that right away' or 'that would be impossible for me', and anything in between.

Here is a chance to record your opinions about all the types of e-learning presented in this book.

The table near the end of the book on page 41 lists all the uses for e-learning that were discussed in the previous section. Read through the table, and tick a box to show whether:

> you already use this type of e-learning;

> you don't do it yet, but you intend to give it a try;

> you don't want to try it yet, but it sounds interesting;

> this type of e-learning just isn't right for you, or may be impossible to implement.

There is also room for you to record decisions about what actions to take next, and to jot down contacts and resources that you might look into. You may not be able to complete these sections yet – but don't worry. You can go back to this table and amend it as you learn more.

As with the rest of this book, you can photocopy the table for your own use or to give to your colleagues, or adapt it to use with learners.

Support providers

This section gives you access to some resources to support e-learning. By using these resources you might make it easier to implement the ideas for e-learning that you have marked for consideration in the ratings table (page 41). You might transform ideas which you had considered impossible into possibilities.

If you find any ideas here which are useful to you, then you can record them in the 'ratings' table.

The table opposite summarises some sources of support, and the particular focus of each. It includes organisations, programmes they provide, and initiatives which have produced useful ideas and resources for you to use (and, in many cases, in which you can get involved). It's in alphabetical order. The website will tell you more in each case.

Short name	Full/alternative name	Focus, website and further information (taken from the website)
ACLearn	Community Learning Resource	e-learning **http://www.aclearn.net/** The Community Learning Resource website supports the sector by providing information, advice and guidance. It is designed to complement the expansion of effective e-learning and related support. It covers: • Learning content • Skills development • Technical guidance • Leadership and management
ALP	Association of Learning Providers	e-learning The organisation, which supports those working in the work-based learning sector, has relevant web pages at http://www.elearningproviders.org/pages/
Ask Butler	Part of the LSN's (see below) e-learning programme	e-learning **http://www.learningtechnologies.ac.uk/ask/users/search.asp** The search engine provided by the LSN e-learning team for • Events • Resources • Examples of e-learning
Becta	British Educational Communications and Technology Agency	Technology in education **http://www.becta.org.uk/** Becta is the Government's lead partner in the strategic development and delivery of its e-strategy for the schools, learning and skills sectors. Becta provides strategic leadership in the innovative and effective use of ICT to enable the transformation of learning, teaching and educational organisations for the benefit of every learner.
Chips	NIACE's *Chips With Everything* magazine	e-learning http://www.aclearn.net/display.cfm?resID=14716 'A newsletter dedicated to the rollout of e-learning into ACL.'
Dysg	Part of the National Assembly for Wales with effect from 1 April 2006. Formerly part of LSDA.	Quality improvement (including e-learning) **http://www.dysg.org.uk/** Dysg's mission is to improve the quality of post-14 education and training. It does this through research to inform policy and practice, through helping to shape and communicate education policy and through improvement and support programmes for organisations that deliver post-14 education and training.
E-Guides	The NIACE E-Guides Programme (and see SDELC below)	e-learning staff development **http://www.niace.org.uk/conferences/TrainingCourses/Eguides2.htm** The programme aims to increase the use of e-learning by

		developing the skills and knowledge of E-Guides to support colleagues from all subjects in their use of technology in teaching and learning. E-Guides will be able to contribute to raising the quality of teaching and learning throughout their organisation. Check via **http://www.niace.org.uk** for current activities.
Ferl	A service from Becta. Previously called 'FE Resources for Learning'	Advice on the use of technology in education **http://ferl.becta.org.uk/index.cfm** An advice and guidance service supporting individuals and organisations in making effective use of ILT within the post-compulsory education sector. Its services cover: • Teaching and learning • Policy and strategies • Technology for e-learning
Futurelab	An independent charity. Was formerly part of NESTA	Technology in education **http://www.futurelab.org.uk/index.htm** Futurelab tries to marry creative and technical innovation with the expertise of learners, teachers and internationally-respected researchers. Through prototypes it creates examples of digital resources that demonstrate the capacities of technology in education and in turn contribute to defining future policies in educational technology.
JISC	JISC e-Learning and Pedagogy programme	e-learning **http://www.jisc.ac.uk/index.cfm?name=elearning_pedagogy** The JISC e-Learning and Pedagogy programme is exploring the complex interactions between teachers, learners and technology. The aim is to help teachers and learners develop a deeper understanding of how they use technology.
Learning and Teaching Scotland	Includes the former Scottish Council for Educational Technology.	Innovation and improvement **http://www.ltscotland.org.uk/** Its remit includes to: • actively promote a climate of innovation, ambition and excellence throughout the Scottish education system; • support teachers, schools and local authorities in improving the quality of education and raising levels of achievement of all learners; • ensure that the curriculum and approaches to learning and teaching, including the use of ICT, assist children and young people in Scotland to develop their full potential.
LSN	Learning and Skills Network. One of the two successor organisations of the Learning and Skills Development Agency (LSDA), and undertaking LSDA's delivery work.	Quality improvement and staff development **http://www.lsneducation.org.uk/** It provides: • Support programmes • Research • Training and consultancy See details of LSN's teacher training e-learning projects at **http://www.learningtechnologies.ac.uk/lsda_tti.asp?area=56**

Learning Technologies	The e-learning and technology programme of the LSN (above).	e-learning professional development **http://www.learningtechnologies.ac.uk/** E-learning staff development resources and activities including: • E-learning continuing professional development • ICT skills • Events • Projects and networks • E-learning resources • E-learning tools and services
Learning and Skills Web		Information and resources **http://www.learningandskillsweb.org.uk/home.do** 'With one single point of access, Learning and Skills Web will find everything you need and, as the site develops and the search engine becomes more refined, you can be assured of speedy access to the best and most relevant information, resources and news.'
NIACE	The National Institute of Adult Continuing Education - England and Wales	NIACE is a non-governmental organisation working for more and different learners **http://www.niace.org.uk/Default.htm** The NIACE ICT and Learning team's aims include: • To carry out research into how ICT and learning can remove barriers embedded in conventional education and training. • To disseminate this research to education and learning providers across sectors, funding bodies, government and policy-makers in order to influence and inform. • To support actively non-conventional approaches to education and learning such as outreach. • To ensure support for excluded and marginalised groups.
NIACE	NIACE good practice guides	Staff development (including e-learning) **http://www.niace.org.uk/Publications/Type/practice.htm** These publications – including 'e-guidelines' – identify and disseminate good practice, and derive from provision rooted in good equal opportunities. They are written and priced accessibly to appeal to a wide range of practitioners. The e-guidelines series provides guidance and support, accessible advice and useful examples of good practice for adult learning practitioners wishing to use digital technology in all its forms to attract and support adult learners.
NIACE	ICT events	e-learning **http://www.niace.org.uk/Publications/F/Firststeps.asp** This is a short straightforward guide for practitioners who are designing and delivering initial information and communication technology events. It covers delivery and learning approaches, methods, initial problems and the learning environment. It provides an introduction to the issues and guidance based on established good practice.

NILTA	AoC NILTA. Formerly the National Information and Learning Technology Association	e-learning **http://www.aoc.co.uk/aoc/aocnilta** The e-learning section of the Association of Colleges which aims to facilitate the active participation of staff working in the lifelong learning sector in the development, use and exploitation of ICT. AoC NILTA does this through enabling the exchange of ideas and expertise, sharing best practice, facilitating partnership and providing access to information, advice and support.
NLN materials	The materials produced by the former NLN (National Learning Network)	e-learning materials **http://www.aclearn.net/display.cfm?page=1000** e-learning materials, designed specifically for adult and community uses, were developed as part of the e-learning strategy for the sector. Some NLN materials (which are still available) are packaged as 'chunks' of learning (learning objects) approximately 15-20 minutes in duration. Providers also have access to the first three rounds of NLN materials, which were designed for further education and sixth form colleges.
Q Projects	The LSN e-learning programme's small-scale staff development project initiative.	e-learning staff development **http://www.learningtechnologies.ac.uk/q.asp?area=38** Q projects are a quick and easy method of introducing staff to the potential of ILT in teaching and learning, through small action-based development projects.
RSCs	JISC regional support centres	Technology and related support **http://www.jisc.ac.uk/index.cfm?name=about_rsc** The JISC Regional Support Centres exist to support learning providers (as identified by their respective funding bodies) and to help them to realise their ambitions in deployment of Information and Communications Technologies (ICT) in order to achieve their organisational mission.
SDELC	NIACE's staff development learning centre	e-learning staff development **http://www.aclearn.net/sdelc** Staff development information, learning activities and resources to support the integration of e-learning in ACL organisations. NIACE developed this staff development e-learning centre to provide staff development training materials online. The content is presented in modules with recommended pathways depending on your role within your organisation. The content includes interactive elements where relevant, and reflection and evaluation exercises. Within each module, all sections are also stand alone to enable a mix and match approach depending on your own objectives.
Teaching and Learning Communities	A service from LSN Northern Ireland	Collaborative online support **http://www.teachingandlearning.org.uk/** The service includes a website (where practitioners can communicate directly with each other and to share content, curriculum development and discuss developments in the sector), printed resources that can be used by individuals or teaching

		teams, and links to the work of LSN and other organisations in Northern Ireland.
TrEACL	NIACE's Technology to Enhance Adult and Community Learning project initiative	e-learning development projects **http://www.aclearn.net/display.cfm?page=951** This initiative (now ended) supported a wide range of innovative projects to enhance learning through the use of technology. The website includes links and project reports.
WON	NIACE wireless outreach networks initiative.	Wireless laptop computers in the community **http://www.niace.org.uk/Research/ICT/WON.htm** An initiative which ran up to 2006 and provided networks of wireless laptop computers for use in increasing access to learning through technology for socially and economically disadvantaged adults in England. The reports about what happened – and useful case studies – are available on the website.

3

Practice

So far we have looked at the potential for e-learning and ideas about using this potential to support your professional activities. This section is about the practice of e-learning. It is about what happens when e-learning is implemented wherever and however you work with learners. It explains what benefits it could bring to you and your learners. The explanations are backed up with research which shows the impact that e-learning can have. But, most importantly, this section is about your practice. It is only when e-learning is integrated into the routines of tutors that it can begin to show any benefits at all.

The most important message to take from this section is that e-learning is not a substitute for you as a tutor, or an independent add-on to your teaching. Instead e-learning is a tool which should be integrated into your teaching activity, and the learning activity of your learners. In other words it is not an easy option, and it does not reduce the importance of the teaching practitioner. The climate of opinion among educationalists is that e-learning will never be a substitute for professional teaching. The human element will always be vital and central. This section is about the human element. Here is a map of this section.

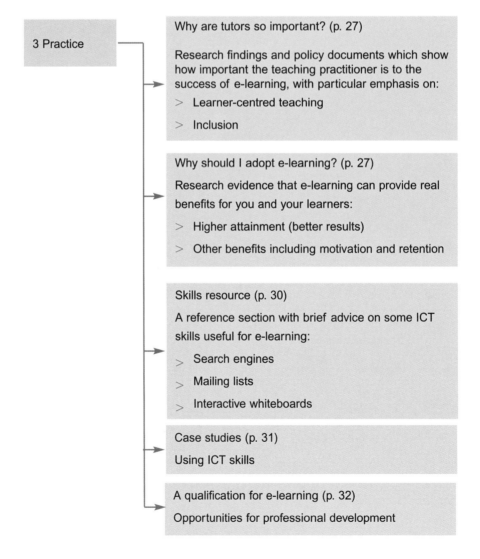

3 Practice

Why are tutors so important? (p. 27)

Research findings and policy documents which show how important the teaching practitioner is to the success of e-learning, with particular emphasis on:
> Learner-centred teaching
> Inclusion

Why should I adopt e-learning? (p. 27)

Research evidence that e-learning can provide real benefits for you and your learners:
> Higher attainment (better results)
> Other benefits including motivation and retention

Skills resource (p. 30)

A reference section with brief advice on some ICT skills useful for e-learning:
> Search engines
> Mailing lists
> Interactive whiteboards

Case studies (p. 31)

Using ICT skills

A qualification for e-learning (p. 32)

Opportunities for professional development

Why are tutors so important?

Researchers have studied the way that e-learning works in practice. There is one message which comes through loud and clear from the research – the contribution of the teaching practitioner is vital. Without this contribution, and in the contexts which concern you and this book, technology can have no impact on learning.

This section is about the research that is available. It will give you the highlights of actual research findings and some pointers to other sources of research which you can read for yourself. It also includes references to some government and related pronouncements which show how e-learning is taken seriously. The section does not quote extensively from the research (if you want to read the original publications we've provided the sources) but, rather, picks out the key findings.

> If you would like to look at the research and key documents in more detail, these links will be useful. Once you reach the various websites you may need to explore them to find the relevant research findings.
>
> Becta's research pages
> **http://partners.becta.org.uk**
>
> Becta's 'what the research says' summaries
> **http://partners.becta.org.uk/index.php?section=rh**
>
> LSN's e-learning research pages are at
> **http://www.lsneducation.org.uk/research** and
> **http://www.learningtechnologies.ac.uk/research**
>
> Some JISC research projects can be found via
> **http://www.jisc.ac.uk**
>
> Earlier LSC sponsored research at
> **http://www.lsc.gov.uk/**
>
> DfES e-strategy for England
> **http://www.dfes.gov.uk/publications/e-strategy/**
>
> The post-16 e-learning strategy and partnership **http://www.becta.org.uk**
>
> Wales: the e-learning country
> **http://www.wales.gov.uk/**
>
> Northern Ireland e-learning partnership
> **http://www.class-ni.org.uk/**
>
> The Scottish e-learning alliance is at
> **http://www.e-learningalliance.org/content.asp?ArticleCode=2**
>
> NIACE ICT research
> **http://www.niace.org.uk/research/ICT/default.htm**

Why should I adopt e-learning?

A practitioner considering the adoption of e-learning isn't interested in 'hype'. He or she is interested in the experiences of other practitioners, and the research evidence. This section will present you with some of the reasons why it is worth adopting e-learning. Why, according to the research, should tutors be keen to use e-learning? We have taken some key and relevant findings from research, which you can find by exploring the sources above, and related this to what tutors think is important.

Learner-centred

One of the most interesting ways in which e-learning can influence your practice is to make it easier for your learners to work independently, at their own pace, or in pursuit of their own interests. It enhances the personal, or learner-centred, aspect of teaching.

The UK government has taken up this idea in its e-strategy (referred to in the box above) with a call for 'personalised learning'. Tutors probably support this, as they have a tradition of helping individuals. But they may also be keen to balance this approach with the undoubted social and educational benefits of belonging to and learning in a group.

Thus, for example, e-learning allows learning in 'bite-sized chunks' so that learners can master something small, be tested on it, and record their achievement (perhaps in an e-portfolio). This means that chunks of learning, provided they fit into some overall coherent approach, can be accredited and rewarded appropriately. So education might be tailored more exactly to an individual learner's needs, although some researchers argue that the full potential of e-learning is not being realised because too much of the pedagogical approach has been transferred unreflectively from didactic traditional teaching.

However some studies suggest that e-learning can help confidence building, motivation and learning, not just delivery of subject knowledge. That depends upon applying technology to assist the achievement of learning objectives, not merely adapting teaching and learning to suit the technology used. It also requires a well-structured approach, proceeding incrementally and allowing for progression, and consideration of individual and group learning styles and preferences. Far from being a substitute for the human side of teaching and learning, e-learning facilities (when they are used properly) should enhance your ability to interact and communicate with your learners.

There is a lot of research about the motivational effects of technology and there is some evidence of improvements in achievement, although the success of individual learners is influenced by their readiness for self-directed learning, their competence with study skills, and their motivation, as well as the learning context.

Human interaction emerges as a key factor in many studies that try to identify critical successful factors for technology. Both online and face-to-face tutoring and peer-to-peer support are identified as important, as is some social interaction. The importance of human interaction highlights a need for staff development so that tutors and others can take into account the changes needed to use e-learning. While there is some evidence of effective staff development initiatives in the UK, it's clear that more work is needed.

Although accessible computer technology has been part of our lives for over twenty years, it is still in its infancy within the span of education and of other resources.

> If you would like to explore whether computers make any 'significant difference' to teaching and learning, take a look at
> **http://www.nosignificantdifference.org/**

Inclusion

Another important aspect of e-learning is that it can be used to include, rather than to exclude. Whether computers end up serving as a barrier to participation by learners of all ages, backgrounds, and abilities, or as a means to include these learners, depends on the contribution of the tutor, and the decisions that he or she makes about how to implement e-learning.

There is much concern about the so-called 'digital divide' and fear that existing participation patterns can be reinforced, as social groups who make most use of technology are those most likely to participate in learning. Some studies draw attention to the problems and barriers to learning or participation that can result when e-learning is poorly implemented. But it seems that the critical success factors for the use of e-learning to improve inclusion and participation include:

> Local availability of technology for communities or individuals that need support

> Use of 'bite sized chunks' of learning

> Presenting opportunities for learners to get on to the 'first rung' of the ladder to make learning more accessible and manageable

> Combining social and technical innovations

> Integrating learning, social and personal development with community development

> Using a range of technologies (e.g. TV, digital video, mobile telephony, games) not just the Internet

> Using assistive technologies for learners with disabilities

> There is more on the 'digital divide' on the Internet including, for example, at
> **http://www.strategy.gov.uk/work_areas/digital _strategy/index.asp**

The use of technology alone cannot overcome issues of exclusion. Nor is the integration of learners with special educational needs guaranteed by the use of technology, and there is a consensus that technology should provide a full range of educational services and alternative learning resources for learners with disabilities and learning difficulties. Research has found that not all current hardware, software, systems, learning tools and online programmes are designed with the varied requirements of people with special educational needs and disabilities in mind. There's more information in the section on page 17.

Attainment

A lot of research illustrates a strong belief by educators and policy makers, in the UK and overseas, that the use of technology in education and training can produce positive benefits for learners and society. It is suggested that e-learning can improve access to and support of learning, motivate learners, improve achievement and increase participation in lifelong learning.

There is some research evidence to support these conclusions, although many educators appear to have been convinced mostly by their own experiences of teaching and learning. Policy makers have based their conclusions partially on observations of the significant role technology has played in changing other sectors of our society and on the willingness of commercial companies to invest in technology. Some of this response is competitive: if we don't do it, others will and we will lose our customers – or learners.

We will leave readers to explore the evidence in the sources in this book, which include lots of case studies of the real benefits for real learners. But we think you will find interesting two sets of important examples which can be found in the references below. They include the wide-reaching results of the use of laptop computers in the community; and the 'transformation projects', which were designed to allow a range of organisations to 'transform' an area of their work by using e-learning.

> The laptops examples are at
> **http://www.niace.org.uk/Research/ICT/WON/c asestudies/Default.htm**
>
> The transformation project reports can be found via
> **http://www.learningtechnologies.ac.uk/transf ormation/default.asp?area=45**

E-learning has been adopted by companies in the private sector, and by public institutions like the National Health Service (NHS) and Ministry of Defence (MoD). Although there are obviously big differences between the training needs of these types of organisation and the needs of most of the post-16 sector, we can look at their experiences as an indication of the types of benefit we could obtain.

Where commercial companies have introduced e-learning approaches to replace traditional training courses direct comparison between the two approaches is possible, providing evidence that e-learning:

> can train more employees quicker;

> can reduce off-the-job time;

> allows standardisation of delivery;

> supports just-in-time and just-what-I-want approaches;

> can result in better knowledge retention by trainees;

> means that application of theory can be reinforced more effectively by the reality of learning in the workplace;

> allows, through simulations and modelling, realistic observation of processes too rapid, too slow or too dangerous to observe in real time;

> breaks down the barriers of stigma which are a common problem in basic skills and ESOL teaching.

> Becta research on the impact of ICT on attainment can be found at
> **http://partners.becta.org.uk/index.php? section=rh**

Other benefits

Here are some of the other benefits that researchers (in the studies above) have found when e-learning is used effectively:

> Learners are motivated to perform better and attend more regularly.

> Learners are more enthusiastic.

> Learners have more self-confidence.

> Learners have access to more than one point of view.

> Learners are encouraged and enabled to be more creative.

> e-learning offers more flexible, modular learning.

> It extends learning outside the classroom.

> It allows people with other commitments (like jobs and childcare) to learn in their spare time.

Skills resource

Search engines

Internet search engines are websites that help you to find the information you need on the Internet. The search engine uses a technology known as a 'web crawler' to look for interrelated data and produce indexes of pages to help searches for specific information.

At the time of writing the most popular and well-regarded search engine is Google.

> Google – **http://www.google.co.uk/** – with the option to restrict your search to UK websites.
>
> If you would like to read more about (more advanced) web searching, have a look at **http://www.ala.org/ala/lita/litaresources/toolkit forexpert/toolkitexpert.htm**
>
> A more dramatic search engine can be found at Google Earth **http://earth.google.com/**
>
> Information about web crawlers and related technologies can be found at **http://en.wikipedia.org/wiki/Web_crawler**

To use a search engine, type a few key words in the box provided on the screen relating to the topic that you want to research. The engine will give you a list of sites that feature those key words. The more carefully and precisely you choose the search terms, the more likely you are to find a useful site.

For a case study on the use of search engines see page 31

Mailing lists

A mailing list is a service which allows a group of subscribers to share emails. If you send an email 'to the list' it will be sent to everyone who has subscribed to the list. And in turn you can read the emails contributed by other subscribers. It's a kind of multi-way conversation by email.

> Find out more about mailing lists at **http://ferl.becta.org.uk/display.cfm?resID=5561**
>
> Find out how to set up a private mailing list at **http://groups.yahoo.com**

Interactive whiteboards

An interactive whiteboard is a large, touch-sensitive board which is connected to a digital projector and a computer. The projector displays the image from the computer screen on the board. The computer can then be controlled by touching the board, either directly or with a special pen. There are a number of manufacturers of interactive whiteboards, offering a variety of specifications and capabilities at a range of prices.

An interactive whiteboard can be used to:

> display web-based resources to the whole class;

> show video clips;

> demonstrate the use of software;

> present learners' work to the rest of the class;

> manipulate text and practise handwriting;

> save notes written on the board for future use;

> teach 'traditionally' or to learn collaboratively.

> 'What the research says' on Interactive whiteboards: **http://www.becta.org.uk/page_documents/res earch/wtrs_whiteboards.pdf**
>
> Case study: use of interactive whiteboards – see page 31

Learning materials

As we have noted several times in this book, computers and other technologies are no use for learning unless there is something to do with them or 'on' them. In other words you and your learners will use them as means to an end – finding information, developing skills and knowledge, and so on. That requires, for example, access to the Internet – or being able to use some appropriate software. This could either be an 'application' such as word-processing or a database, or it could be the e-learning equivalent of another medium such as a text book or a film; it's material which can be used for teaching and learning.

> We've given you lots of sources of materials in other parts of this book (for example see page 12); you may also wish to have a look at some of the following:
>
> **http://www.learningtechnologies.ac.uk/resources.asp?area=7**
>
> **http://www.intute.ac.uk**
>
> **http://www.bbc.co.uk/learning/subjects/adult_learning.shtml**
>
> Materials which schools can access are at
> **http://www.curriculumonline.gov.uk/Default.htm**

If you are keen to see lots of materials and other resources on show you may wish to visit one of the big e-learning exhibitions.

> Examples of e-learning shows include:
>
> **http://www.bettshow.co.uk/**
>
> **http://www.education-show.co.uk/**

Case studies

Jenny

Jenny was a tutor in family history and was planning to work in Liverpool. She wanted to find out about related local resources before she moved. She went to the Google search engine, and typed 'family history Liverpool' and immediately got over seven million results. Near the top of the list of sites that Google found Jenny discovered contact details for local family history groups, and details of resources available in a local library. It took less than a minute from the time she started up the Internet to find this information.

Matthew

Matthew Pugh, a lecturer at Bournemouth and Poole College, has used interactive whiteboards with a variety of learners, including those with a severe learning difficulty or disability. He has found that all learners benefit from their interactivity and large screen size and that they learn at a greater rate than those not using the whiteboards. In particular, he identifies the power of images and the capacity for collaboration as significant in whiteboards' impact on learning, as in the following examples:

> A Bangladeshi learner who never normally took part in class discussions was so inspired by the web-based images from her homeland that she used the whiteboard to present to her classmates for 15 minutes.

> A group planning a trip used the Internet and the whiteboard's digital flipchart feature to find out costs and directions and write an itinerary. The whiteboard allowed the learners to take control of their learning. At the end of the lesson the work was printed off, ensuring that each learner had a record of their achievements.

Participation is further encouraged by the use of an infrared keyboard which can be passed round the room. In this way all learners can contribute, regardless of mobility. Matthew Pugh, however, notes that the novelty of using the technology can wear off so a range of approaches is necessary to maintain interest.

(This case study is taken from Becta's What the research says publication on Interactive whiteboards.)

> Have a look at the video case studies of using e-learning materials at
> **http://www.nln.ac.uk/materials/default.asp**

Opportunities for professional development

Tutors who have taken an interest in e-learning, will want to develop their skills and may wish to obtain a qualification or accreditation of their skills. Of course there are many traditional qualifications, such as A-Levels taken by evening class, or Open University degrees, and postgraduate qualifications offered part time by your local university. If you want to take the academic route you might like to look at technological courses, or educational courses which offer modules in the use of technology. There are also some vocational qualifications which are relevant to this area, and represent a significant investment of effort and time, but would not require the long-term commitment of an academic degree course.

Change

One certainty is that e-learning is an area of constant change and challenge – for technologists and for tutors. We think that the kinds of professional development suggested by this book, and supported by the associated resources, will help staff in the sector to cope with these changes and the challenges. Involvement in professional networks and forums will always be useful.

What accreditation is currently available for e-learning?

Joint Examining Board (JEB)

Level 3 Certificate in Educational use of ICT.

Level 3 Certificate in Delivering Learning using a VLE.

> See **http://www.jeb.co.uk**

LeTTOL

LeTTOL (Learning To Teach On-Line) is an online distance education course aimed at teachers, lecturers, trainers and content developers who wish to transfer their existing skills to an online environment. It is accredited by the National Open College Network.

> See **http://www.sheffcol.ac.uk/lettol/index.html**

ITQ

ITQ is a unit-based IT user qualification and training package that has been created to ensure staff are trained in the IT skills they need to carry out their roles. It is primarily aimed at ICT users and not professional IT staff and allows different units to be taken at different levels. LSN has produced an ITQ resource pack, which has been created by practitioners in the post-16 sector to support the development of staff ICT user skills. It has been aligned to the new ITQ qualification to allow both teaching staff and those who directly support teaching and learning to acquire those skills in context.

> Details from **http://itq.e-skills.com/** and **http://www.learningtechnologies.ac.uk/itqss/home.htm**
>
> NIACE is publishing an ITQ workbook. Details on the NIACE website at **http://www.niace.org.uk**

Definitions

What do all these terms mean?

This section presents you with a short 'dictionary' of technical and e-learning terms. Read it through, or keep it as reference, and look up terms as you encounter them in the rest of this guide.

Alternatively just go straight to
http://www.niace.org.uk/Research/ICT/Jargon buster.htm

or Learning Circuits at
http://www.learningcircuits.org/glossary.html

IT, ICT, ILT – what's the difference?

IT

IT stands for Information Technology. This term is used mainly to refer to the computer equipment used to process data and deliver information.

ICT

ICT stands for Information and Communications Technology. This refers to the combination of computers and connectivity. By linking computers and telecommunications we have access to systems and services like email and the Internet. (People in the schools sector sometimes use the term 'ICT' in the same way that the term 'ILT' is used in post-16 education, to mean the use of technology in the classroom.)

ILT

ILT stands for Information and Learning Technology. This term is used in parts of post-16 education to refer to the use of computers and other technology to support learning and the management of learning.

Does it matter?

Well, as you have seen, we chose to use the above terms as little as possible and instead opt for:

e-learning

Lifelong Learning UK, the body which sets the job standards for the professionals in the sector says that e-learning is learning supported or enhanced through the application of information and communications technology. It also says that ILT = e-learning plus e-leadership.

You can read more at
http://www.lifelonglearninguk.org/standards/s tandards_index.html

The term 'e-learning' is now used frequently to describe the use of technology for learning and to help manage learning. The definition of e-learning adopted in Wales is: 'Using electronic technology to deliver, support and, ultimately, transform teaching and learning.'

The Learning Circuits website (above) defines e-learning as a 'Term covering a wide set of applications and processes, such as Web-based learning, computer-based learning, virtual classrooms, and digital collaboration. It includes the delivery of content via Internet, intranet/extranet (LAN/WAN), audio- and videotape, satellite broadcast, interactive TV, CD-ROM, and more'.

All the terms overlap to some extent – the important thing is that you know what you mean!

Other terms in use

Blended learning
Combining e-learning with more traditional learning styles. This is probably the most popular way to make use of e-learning. For example, learners may spend half a lesson finding things out on the Internet, and the second half of the lesson in a guided discussion.

C&IT
C&IT stands for Communications and Information Technology. You will sometimes see this term used instead of ICT, particulary within the Scottish education system.

DEL
'Distributed and Electronic Learning' is another term for e-learning sometimes used in adult and higher education. 'Distributed' learning is not confined within a particular learning location; connectivity can enable learners to learn in a wide range of locations, including their own homes.

Telematics
This term is sometimes used instead of ICT, particularly in projects supported by the EU.

TBT (technology-based training)
TBT is training, typically for adult learners, and typically for professional or vocational purposes. It is delivered using computers, with or without connectivity to the Internet or a local network. An example would be training for nurses, where they learn about new drug treatments, by reading text on the computer screen, and then being tested in an online multiple choice examination.

Two types of TBT are CBT (computer-based training), which is delivered by a single computer without using an Internet connection, and WBT (web-based training) where the learner connects to a remote website that delivers content and perhaps online tests.

Some more technical terms

Assistive technology
This means technology which is used to assist people – typically with a disability – who might otherwise have problems with some of the activities of learning. An example would be software that 'reads' text out loud for a learner with sight difficulties.

Blog (weblog)
An extension of having a personal website, it consists of regular journal-like entries posted on a web page for public viewing. Blogs usually contain links to other websites along with the thoughts, comments and personality of the blog's creator.

Broadband
Broadband connectivity means computer connections that are so powerful they can send high-density information, such as a video clip, at high speed. Broadband connections can be so powerful that a whole classroom of users could send and receive information at the same time. Without broadband connectivity, Internet usage can be quite slow.

Connectivity
Connectivity is the ability to join computers together over short or long distances so that they can communicate information. Networks, modems, and telephone lines (or other telecommunications connections) are elements necessary for connectivity.

e-portfolio
Becta defines e-portfolios as:

> The (electronic) process and services through which outcomes of learning and assessment are recorded.

> The process and services through which outcomes and evidence of learning are used to support transitions between phases of learning and career development across a lifetime.

> A process of presenting digital evidence of

progress and achievement to self and others.

> A process to support reflection on learning through creating a personal narrative of progress.

> **See for example**
> **http://www.recordingachievement.org/**

Extranet

This is a private computer network belonging to an organisation but accessible to identified outsiders – such as customers or learners.

> See **http://en.wikipedia.org/wiki/Extranet**

Intranet

This is an organisation's own private internal network (its own 'web') restricted to inside use.

Learning objects

Traditionally, learning content comes in large 'chunks', for example, a lesson which will take an hour or more, or a text book which will take many hours to read. Learning objects are much smaller chunks of learning. They:

> are self-contained – each learning object can be used independently;

> are reusable – a single learning object may be used in multiple contexts for multiple purposes;

> can be grouped together to make lessons and even complete courses.

If learning content material is split into self-contained 'objects' and assigned to learners, the course becomes more flexible, and learners can work at their own pace. Technology helps teachers to make use of learning objects, typically through a VLE (virtual learning environment).

Learning platform

This is a single online location from which course resources can be made available to learners. These resources can include course materials, communications tools such as email, and a storage area for learners' work.

Learning platforms can be developed using a range of technology components, such as an intranet or extranet, or a virtual learning environment.

Managed learning environment (MLE)

A managed learning environment is a bigger, typically institution-wide, software system, which links the VLE (see below) used to deliver a particular course to the information system within which that course operates. So, an MLE may keep track of learners as they move between classes and courses, and it may offer management-level information to do with course attendance, learner retention rates, exam registration etc.

Multimedia

Multimedia means the combination of different ways of conveying information. Text, sound, pictures, animation and video clips may all combine in a multimedia presentation. Computers make all forms of multimedia more usable in the classroom, and connectivity gives access to multimedia content over the Internet. If all these media are available but not combined together for a specific purpose, the more correct term is 'multiple media'.

Virtual learning environment (VLE)

A virtual learning environment is a software system that gives learners access to learning content, typically in the form of learning objects (see above). In a typical VLE the learner will 'log on', work through a series of connected short learning sessions, and perhaps take diagnostic tests to confirm progress. The system may record the learner's progress and provide information for the tutor.

Materials for you to use

The questionnaire

You can photocopy these pages before use, and revise your e-learning profile at a later date or help colleagues to create their own profiles. Answer the questionnaire below, marking the answer that most closely represents your personal circumstances. Then transfer the answers to the grid which follows.

1. What level of personal and home access do you have to computer facilities, connectivity and software?

    a)   You don't have access to a computer at home for your own personal use.

    b)   You have use of a computer with limited facilities and no Internet or email access.

    c)   You have a computer which is connected to the Internet. You have email. You have access to more than just word-processing software.

    d)   You have personal access to a computer with extra features such as broadband connectivity, specialist software, multimedia editing.

2. How many of your learners have access to computer facilities at home? What about email and the Internet?

    a)   Few of your learners have access to computers at home.

    b)   Some of your learners have use of computers, but you can't rely on all learners having access, and it wouldn't be fair to expect them to use computer facilities for set assignments. (Also pick this option if you are not sure about learners' computer access.)

    c)   Almost all your learners have some access to computers outside of the classroom.

    d)   All of your learners have computer access and connectivity, they can send and receive emails and browse the Internet.

3. What are the computer facilities like at the place where you teach?

    a)   There are no computer facilities available at the premises where you teach.

    b)   There are limited computer facilities, for example one per classroom, or a small number in the library/resource centre.

    c)   There are enough computers available that you could set a classroom activity.

    d)   There are good computer facilities in the classroom, with 'extras' such as a network, a fast Internet connection, specialist software etc.

4 How much do you know about using computers for personal or teaching use?

    a)   You have never used a computer, and wouldn't know where to start.

    b)   You use the computer for straightforward activities like word-processing and sending simple emails.

    c)   You can browse the Internet with confidence, you can use a range of computer facilities or software packages, or use more than the basic features of a package.

    d)   You have good computer skills, and you are confident that you could develop new skills as you need them.

The answers

Now fill in your answers in the grid. Draw a ring round the letter that corresponds with your answer to each question.

e-learning potential	Low	Moderate	High	Very high
1 Personal	a	b	c	d
2 Learner	a	b	c	d
3 Institutional	a	b	c	d
4 Skills	a	b	c	d

We used this profiling system with our case study examples on page 4 at the beginning of the book. Here are some examples of how to complete the profile.

You can join up the letters you have circled to find your e-learning profile. Or you can shade in the boxes to give a clearer picture.

e-learning potential	Low	Moderate	High	Very high
1 Personal	a	b	c	d
2 Learner	a	b	c	d
3 Institutional	a	b	c	d
4 Skills	a	b	c	d

e-learning potential	Low	Moderate	High	Very high
1 Personal	a	b	c	d
2 Learner	a	b	c	d
3 Institutional	a	b	c	d
4 Skills	a	b	c	d

And remember – e-learning involves more than computers. Even if you and your learners currently don't have great computer access or skills you may still be able to make use of other technologies like digital cameras or digital video or mobile phones.

Electronic communication quiz

There are no right and wrong answers – and no prizes – but you may wish to photocopy and try this quiz, and use it with colleagues and learners to see how much technology has entered your life. When you have finished it, compare the answers with others – and with your profile (page 38) or your ratings score (page 41).

You and the Internet	
Have you used the Internet in the past month? YES/NO	
What have you used it for in the last month?	
Finding information	
Learning something	
Buying something	
If so, what?	
Booking a holiday	
Anything else?	
How often do you go online?	
Do you use email?	
How often do you check you e-mails?	
What would you miss most if the Internet disappeared overnight?	
Your learners and the Internet	
Do they use the Internet?	
For the above reasons?	
Why else?	
Other technology	
Do you have a mobile telephone?	
How often do you use it?	
To make calls or send texts?	
To take photographs or video clips?	
Did you add your own ring tone?	
Do you have a digital still or video camera?	
Do you edit or print the photographs?	
How do you store the results?	
On a computer or a CD or elsewhere?	
Do you have digital television?	
If so, what system? (Freeview, satellite or cable)	
Do you record programmes?	
What system do you use to do this?	
What use do you make of the remote control hand set?	

Teaching and e-learning quiz

This photocopiable quick quiz is designed to help you think about how you get the ideas for your teaching – and how big a part technology plays in this.

1. **In the subject you teach how important is:**

    a) **Up-to-date information?** (very important / quite important / not very important)

    If 'very or 'quite' give an example:

    b) **Opinions,** academic research, and theories? (very important / quite important / not very important)

    If 'very or 'quite' give an example:

    c) The **experience of practitioners?** (very important / quite important / not very important)

    If 'very or 'quite' give an example:

    Give another example of a piece of subject knowledge that you might need to find out to support your teaching in the future:

2. **Where do you find the above information and ideas?**

    a) From colleagues? Give an example:

    b) From books and other print material? Give an example:

    c) From the Internet or other electronic sources? Give examples:

3. **How do your learners react to the above?** Give examples

    a) They enjoy using technology:

    b) They find information on the Internet:

    c) They seem to benefit in other ways from the use of technology:

    d) They prefer other approaches to teaching and learning:

Record your ratings

Photocopy these pages and then use them to tick as appropriate and give as much information as you can about whether, and how far, e-learning has become part of your repertoire as a teacher.

	I do this	I intend to do this from now on	I am interested, but I won't do it right now	This would be impossible for me	Actions to take	Resources I can use
Presenting content to your learners						
Communicating with learners outside lessons						
Expanding your own knowledge						
Learners finding out						
Learners working in the classroom						
Learners working at home						
Learner platforms						
Class administration						